What do you see?

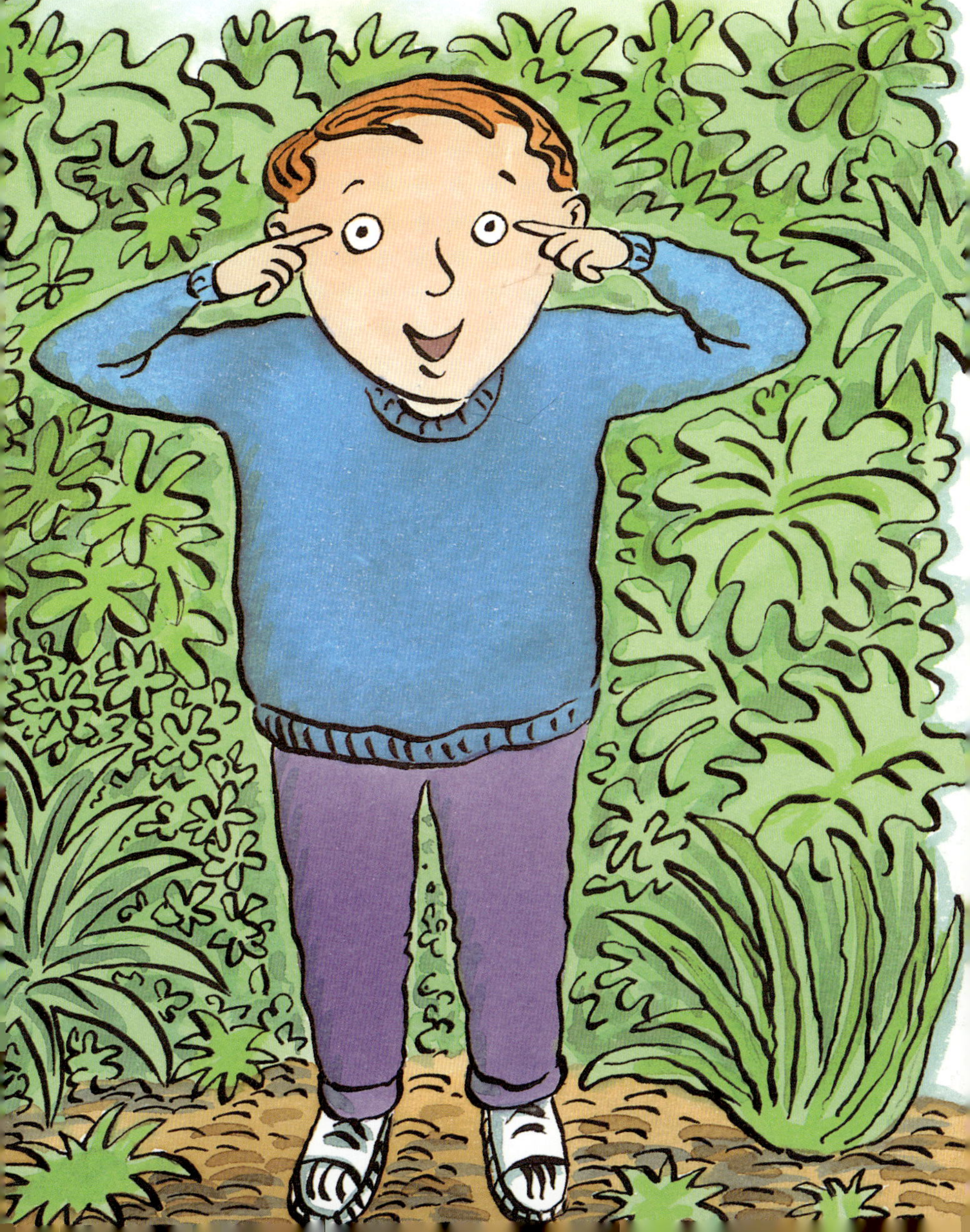

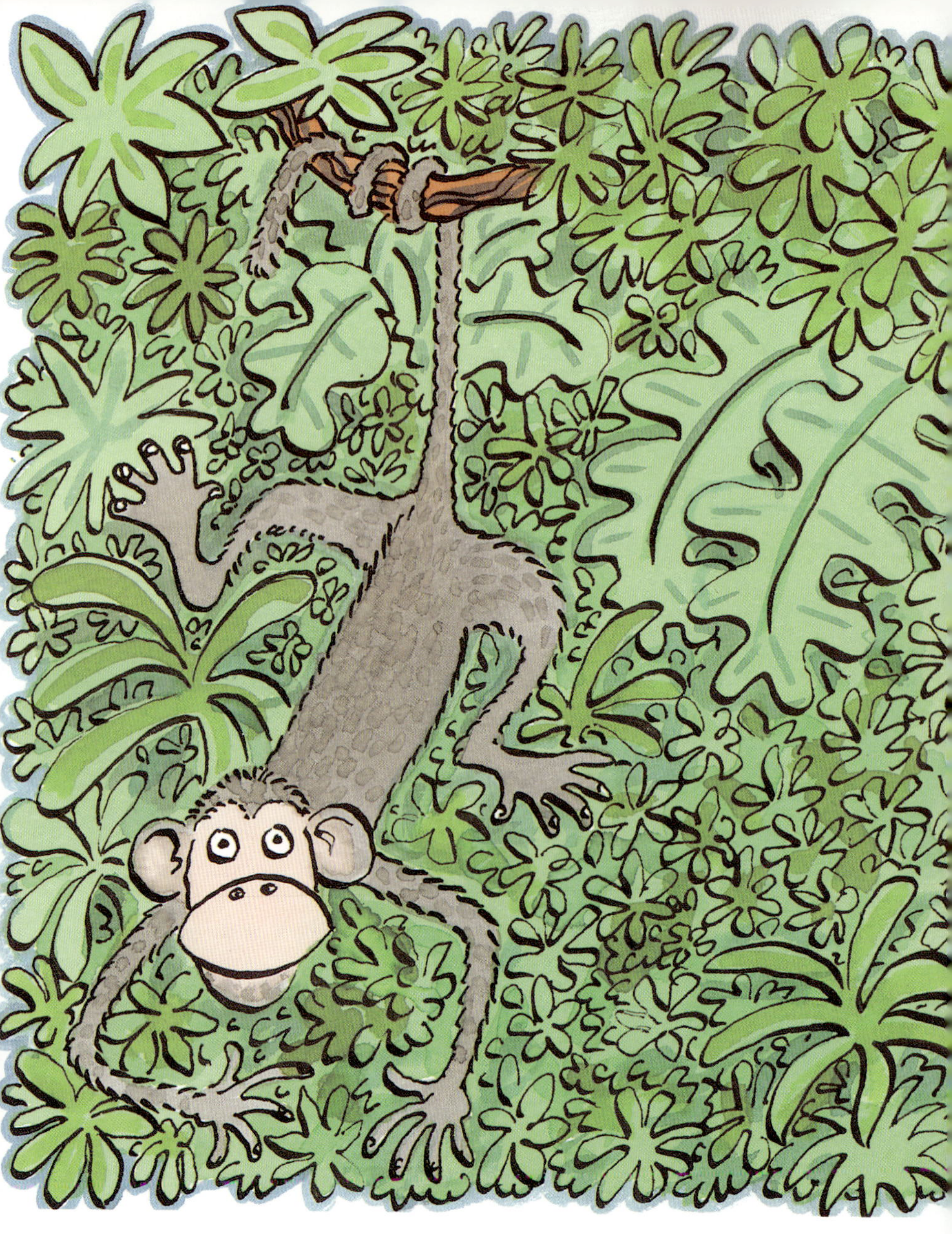

I see one monkey.

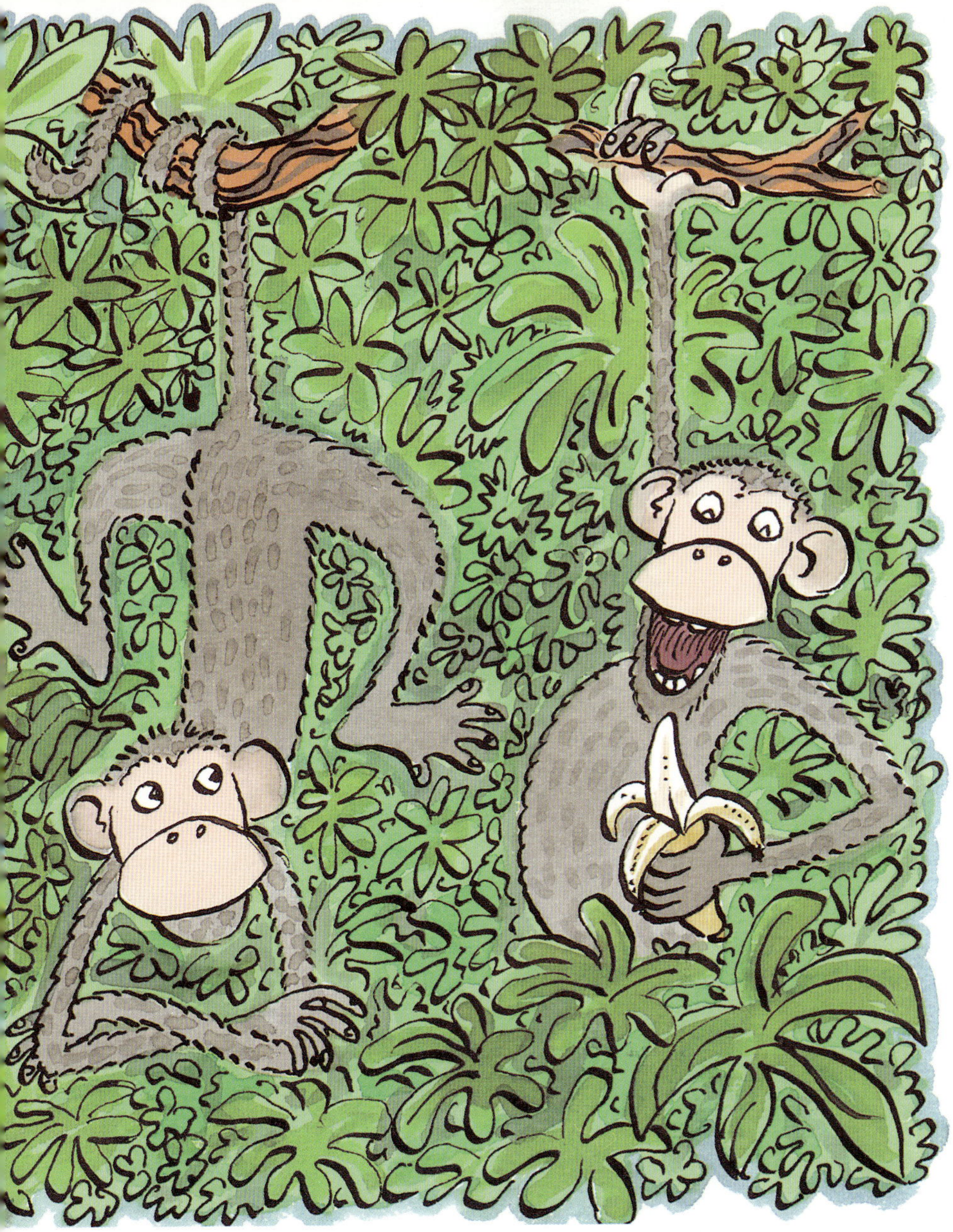

No, I see two monkeys.

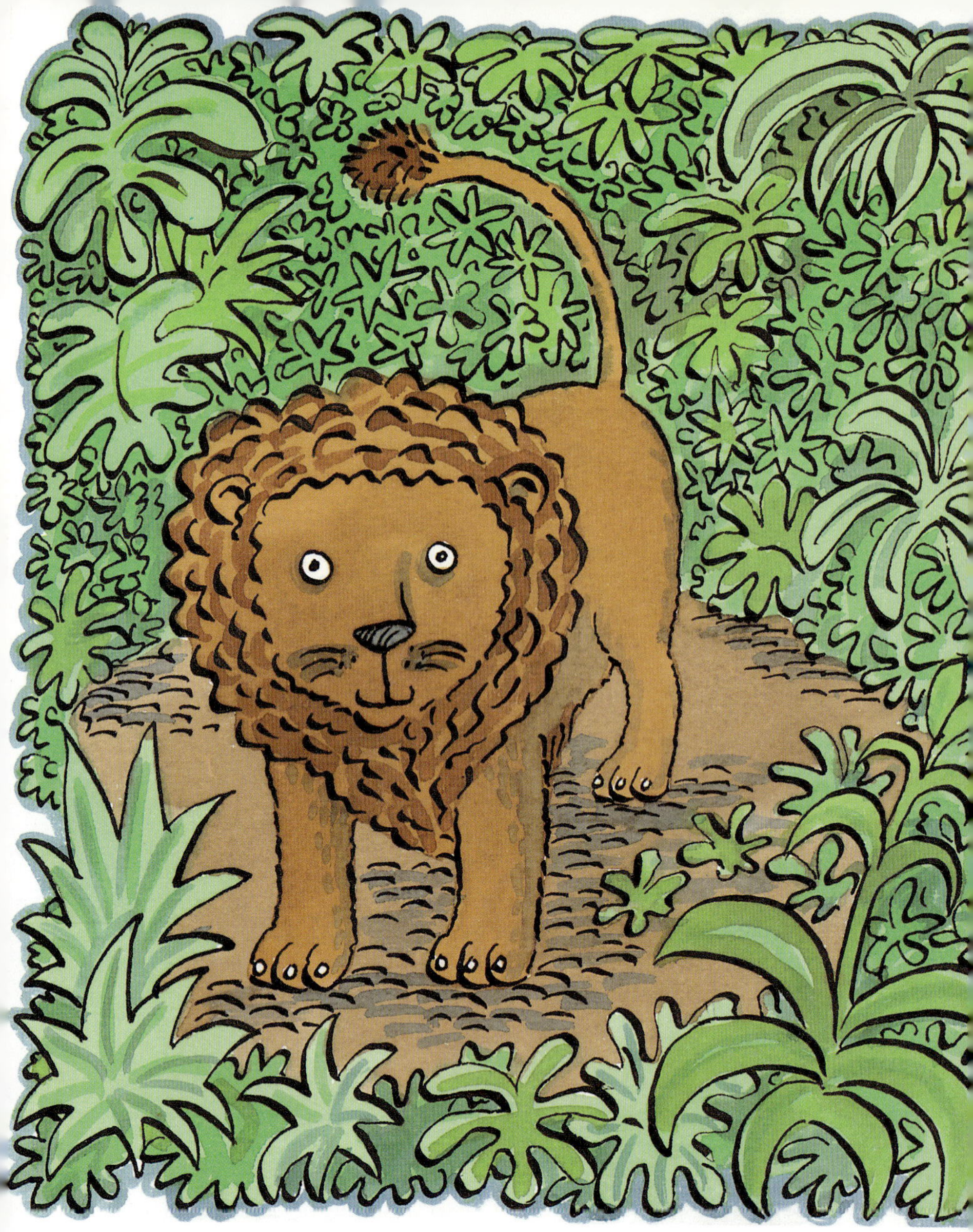

I see one lion.

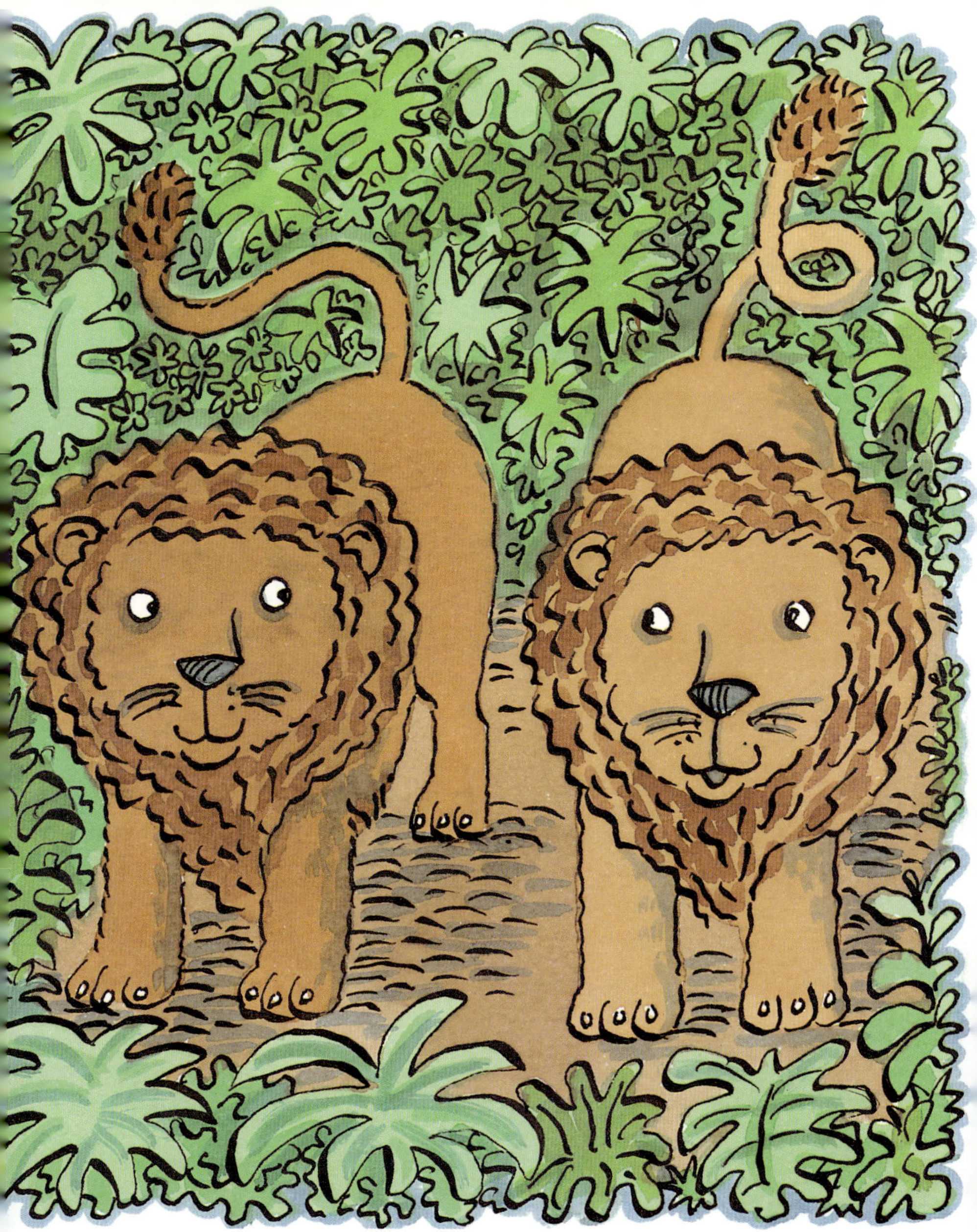

No, I see two lions.

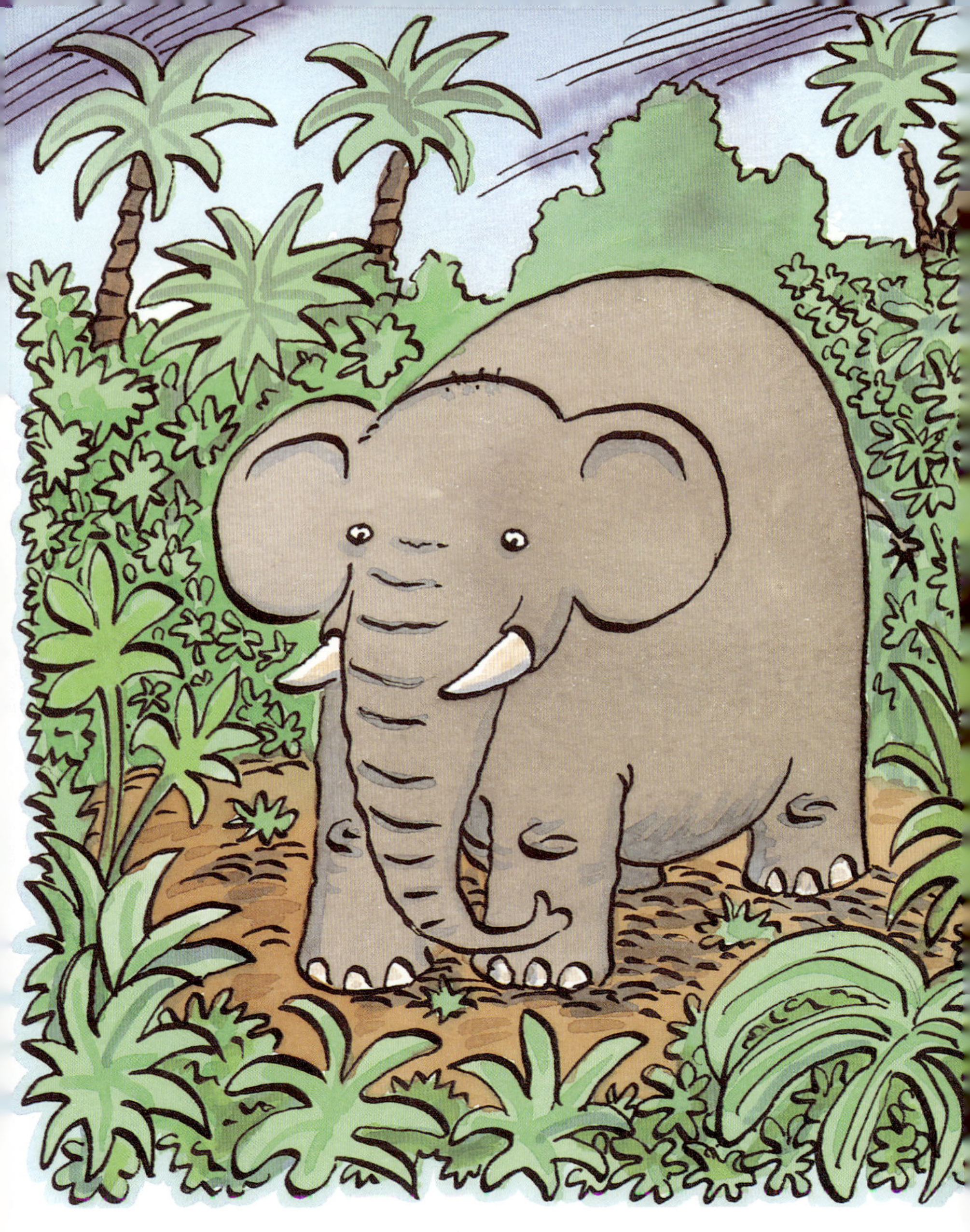

I see one elephant.

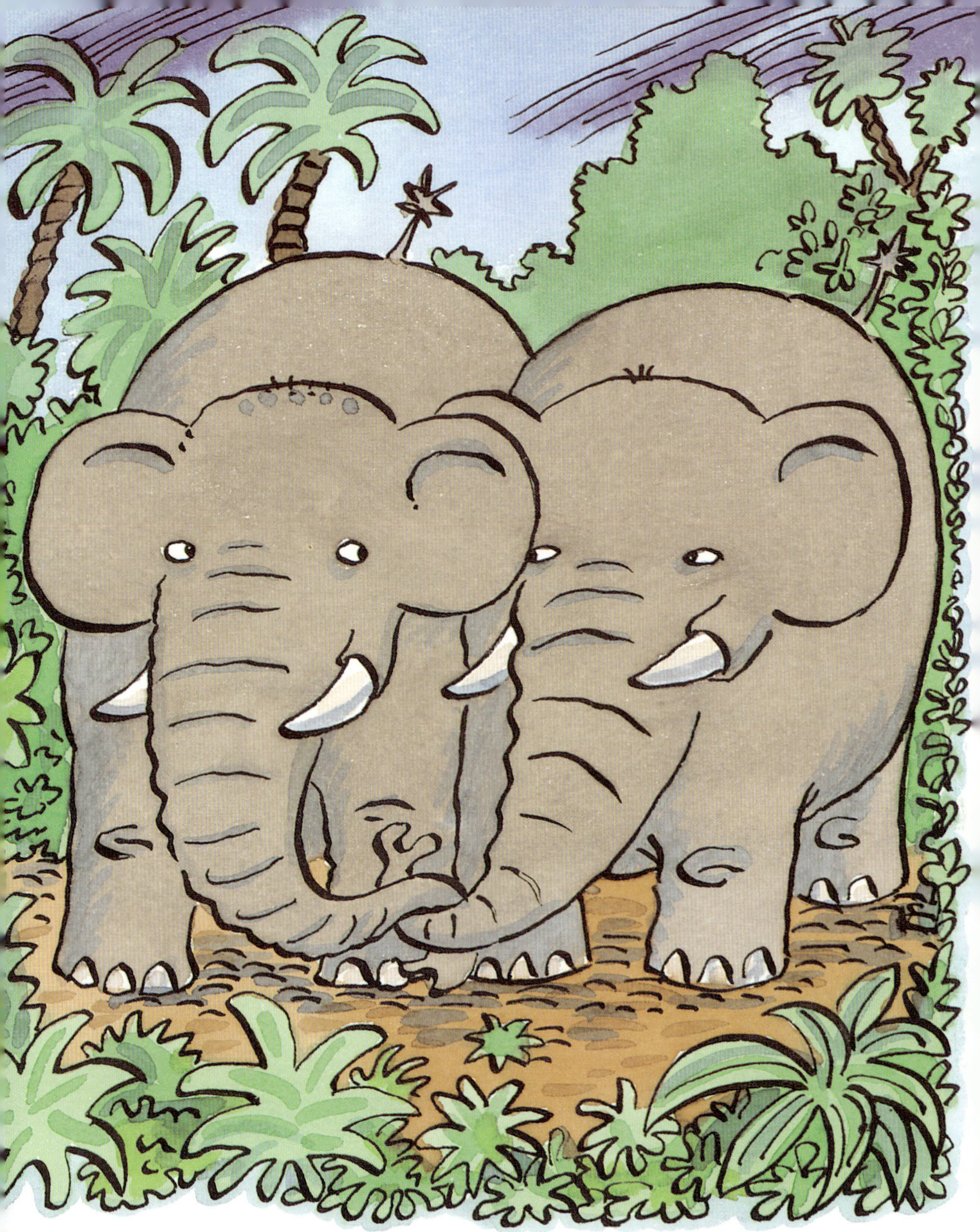

No, I see two elephants.

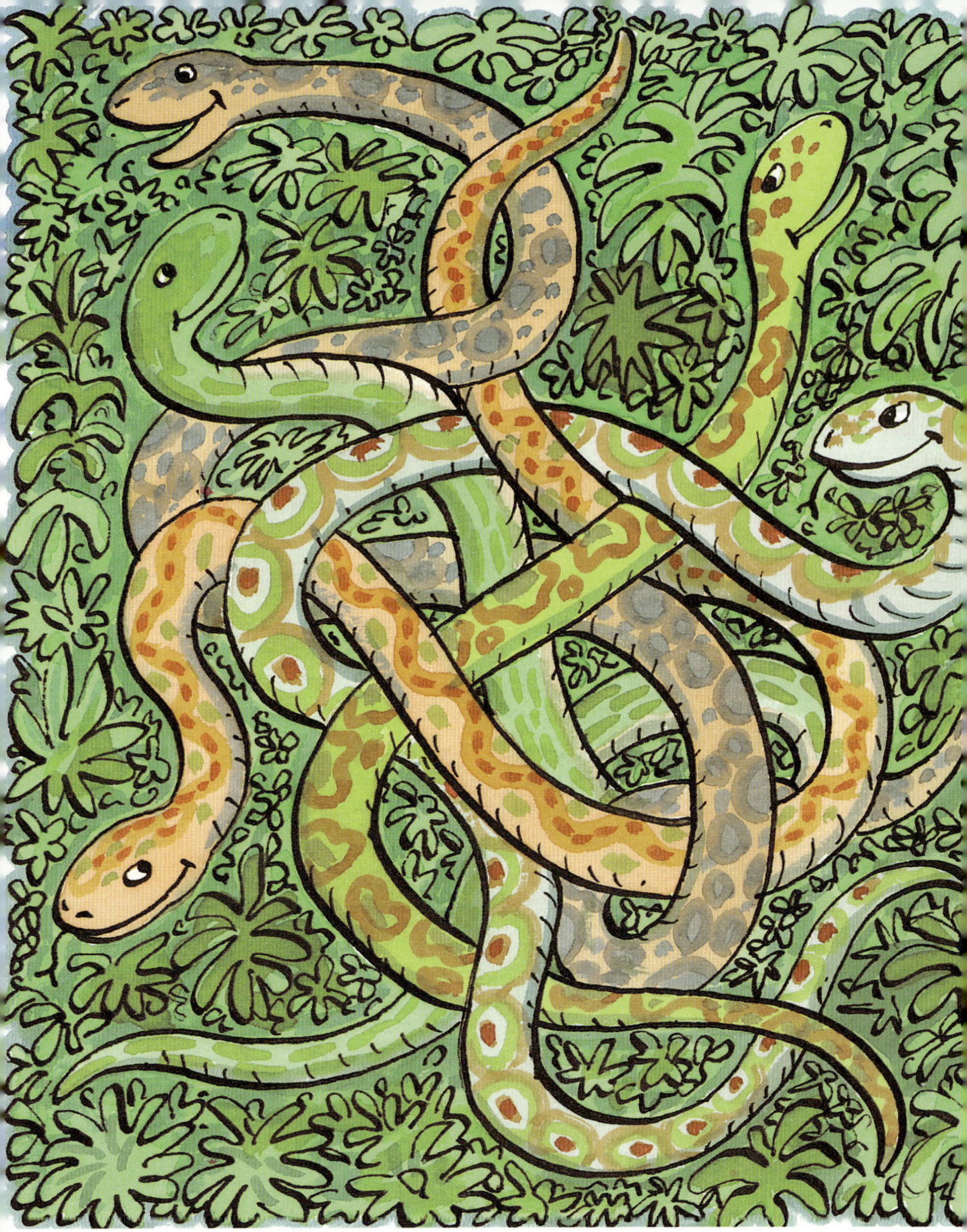

I see lots and lots of snakes. Sssssss!